Why We Keep Breathing

a book of poems

by

Peter James Craig

ISBN: **1884178995**
ISBN-13:**978-1884178993 (*Kairos Center*)**

Cover design by Peter James Craig

*All of these poems were written by Peter
between August 10, 2007, and August 29, 2010,
and are generally displayed chronologically.*

~

To visit Peter's site, go to
www.essentialunion.com

To connect on facebook, go to
facebook.com/pages/essential-union/

To contact Peter, send an email to
rumisroses@gmail.com

~

*To deepen your poetic experience,
inhale, apply, and diffuse therapeutic grade essential oils.*
http://www.essentialunion.com/essential-oils.html

Everything you see has its roots in the unseen world. The forms may change, yet the essence remains the same. Every wonderful sight will vanish; every sweet word will fade, but do not be disheartened. The source they come from is eternal, growing, branching out, giving new life and new joy. Why do you weep? The source is within you and this whole world is springing up from it!

~ Rumi

Contents

Book III ~ The World of Love

Epilogue

To everyone -

Thank you for being alive!

Prologue

ॐ

Eyes of the Sun

And she walked away.

I turned around and saw the vines stretching into the sky, the jungle now redolent with the rich aroma of flowers; my vision bursting with newfound color.

And I took the first step - with grace, with ease, with open eyes and ears.

Suddenly the earth had come alive - I could hear the whizzing and whirring sounds of a hidden world, before so far away from my humanness, now nestling deeper within me than I had ever known.

My heart became the beating drum of nature. I felt the movement of every being and nonbeing, of every rock and tree, every butterfly and coiled snake breathing in and out, being born and dying. The world moved through me, and I was the world. Every footstep echoed through the fabric of the universe. Every breath gave rise to the world and shook it apart. Every thought lived through my senses so that I became what I saw and touched and tasted - that space between became nothing.

I became everything and nothing at once.

All the ideas I had learned, the philosophies, the conversations, the arguments, the building up - *burned in the fire of my new eyes.*

I no longer needed an explanation. I was no longer searching, for anything. I looked back on my life in an instant - I saw the people, the stories, the ravines that carved such sadness and anger, and saw past all of it. I saw past the violence of trying to become something.

I divorced the economy of men
and married the movement of being.

I broke free from the circle
and became the drum.

I opened
like the eyes of the sun.

I became light
like sun-rays breathe through a nun.

I unfurled my wings
and ripped the roots
to one:

I am her walking away.
I am her muscles, her sadness, and her freedom.
I am her unknowing.

I am her.
There is no difference.

Only,
a mirror.

Book 1

~

An Invitation

ॐ

I am an Invitation

I am an invitation.

Now each time I part my lips or move through space,
I invite the world into me
as I invite the world to receive me.

I am an invitation -
To love
and open up!

Like flowers,
like wine,
like good times,

I keep opening,
we keep opening,

I keep breathing, saying
Come, come
to this new world we are loving into!

Let us watch how
all the whispering, all the hungry eyes,
all the passion of the world! Is squeezed into
one breath -

Come.

Come to me.
Come to your longing.
Let us treat our longing by loving.
So that your longing becomes only
the pain of too much joy -

Like birth!
Like the freedom of forgiveness!
Like letting go of

every
single
barrier

from you blowing wide open
the doors of the world

that before hid
all the love in the universe!

Love on all Sides

No one is against love,
but many do not understand it.

No one is against peace,
but to some it holds hands with war.

No one is against life,
but many practice death.

Man does not despise his greater self,
but fears it because he suffers.

One who embraces shallowness and violence
polarizes the heart,
turning mind against body, breath, and soul.

The hunter sharpens his concentration yet aims foul.
He spies in the wrong field and kills his neighbor.

The world has gotten lost
in the name of love.

Verily,
in the name of love
it will be found!

We pretend to be heroes searching for the Holy Grail,
but we are fakes who rarely rise above the haze.

Love is lost
when people take sides.

To take sides is to support something
because you are near it.

Like children we take to the streets,
with or against the next war,
unaware that either way,
love will be flung aside.

To truly support is to love,
but we can never commit.

We cannot commit because we are
afraid to invest everything we have.

Love is limitless
and therefore free.
It cannot be bargained with.

We must accept its offer
or wander the streets of sin.

To *sin* means
being away from the presence of God.

God is a fancy name
for love.

Babies live this wisdom,
but we are too tired for their games.

We have grown old
and our scars, like compromises,
still haunt us.

Turn to the sun.
Again and again,
turn.

We cannot escape the heat,
but only quench its rays.

Do not think,
but *love*.
There will be time to argue later.

Now is the time
to *love*,

and by loving
act,

and by acting,
heal the world.

Say Yes

Yes
is this:

Surrendering to the present moment.

I swear there's nothing sexier
than feeling the essence of the universe pouring into you.

Whether it's the sun on your skin,
the water at your feet,
or making love under an open sky.

The universe pours out constantly!
It shouts *yes!* at every crossing.

So reach out,
reach out to me,
and say *yes*.

When you were First Ignited

When the body feels alive
it sings, or dances, or moans.
I heard them all. I felt them all.

I brought the heart's longing into focus
then gave it away for joy.

Joy in life.
Joy in the curves of compassion
that make up the essence of being human.

To be intimate.
To be a lover,
yet a stranger.

I am bound to roam in and out of homes,
yet I will never leave them.

For loving
is remembering,
and remembering
is going back,

somehow,
even if only in the mind,

to say thank you.
And to say bless you.

And to kindle the fire of love
deeper,

deeper than the way
you felt when

you
were
first

ignited!

Stretching You

My intelligences
stretch out
like your body,

enlivening every
nook and cranny
of your being.

That way,
no room for forgetting
or leaks in the roof.

My house can
winter the stormiest days
your heart will ever see.

This house contains so many mansions
that you couldn't dance wildly enough
to ever escape!

Intoxicated with joy,
oneness makes love
to infinity.

What are you waiting for?
Unfurl yourself!

Unveil
those wings
and breasts
and sing!

Listen

Listen
to the sound
of your voice.

Sometimes
I hear you weep
and retch and moan,

the sound of your voice
like separation from
love.

Sometimes
I hear you laugh
and smile and sigh,

and the sounds
sweep me into
your love.

Listen
to *this*,
oh beautiful soul.

I am in the state of love
such that
we've run out of time!

To *wait,*
to *pretend,*
to not live so *wildly* and *infinitely*
and *nakedly* such that we

16

seduce the world
into undressing!

Into dropping the veils
that carve all the sadness of this world.

And we make love to the sadness
and the new gladness
from letting go!

The world shakes and laughs -
a new birth
in an ancient universe.

Imagine!
An ancient castle
on the isle of your wanting,

with all the honey and sweet bodies
for you to drench your longing.

Imagine!
The most beautiful place in the world.
Live into it now.

Love yourself there!

Dedicate your life
to uncovering the mysteries of beauty!

Take time to get to know yourself -
past the glamorous illusions
and the lies we wear,
and come to the center.

Come to the heart
of the matter,

which is to
*love more than
you can bare!*

- Love incites you to
get so stirred,
so ragged and human -

You strip off
all of your clothes
and become one with the jungle!

The jungle of love
makes you so wild,
so captivatingly beautiful,

that I can't help but fall to my knees
and invite you
to make love with me!

Light in a Bowl

We disappear
then come to life
like wandering fireflies
signaling -

I'm *here*! Then *here*, then -
doesn't matter, the spot.

Feel the spirit
and your direction
will become clear -

A straight line in the sand
that ends up at your lover's door!

There is only one house.
There is only one guest -
you, the *wild lover*.

The *wild lover* is a guest
in the house of the *Be-loved*,
of *that which is loved*.

More like a prisoner,
the way the wild lover
hangs like art,
chained to the Be-loved's wall.

Before rotting away
in the dark dungeon,
the lover *cultivates inner light!*

The Be-loved torments His guests,
wanting only zealous madmen
vying to kill Him,

so He can turn their rage
into a sacred canopy
that burns holes
in the oppressive lies
of our world!

This rage is so full of light,
it uplifts every loving effort
and opens the door to another universe.

~

All the attempts at
holding back our love,
all the illusory barriers,

become empty,
nothing but
light in a bowl.

This light
glows at angles and edges,
whispering, *come,*
look at it this way,

maybe something will open up
and cause a new world
to leap from your soul!

Kiss the Sky

I want her
to want me.

I want her
to *desire my presence.*

Oh I like them all,
but certain curves and worlds
pull you in, they pull me in

to the center of the chest,
to the root of the sexiest
ounce of soul that rocks you full!

I am a hungry lion.
I hunt not just for the pleasure of the flesh,
but for the unveiling of the rest.

I will tear your veils to pieces!
I will rip away your longing to the core!

So that you undress,
slip into a more delicate state
than ever before.

And for the first and fiftieth time,
you feel alive,
and beating with the silent heart
of the lover and maker of the universe,

can you bring that back?

Back to our world of bodies
and wooing,
of hustling and moving,

to create a new world
that demands love
beyond any one person's doing?

Whispering, wanting.
Whispering, wanting

a *love empire*
with bodies
molded from fire!

When light meets the right light,
it burns away
your matter's pain.

So *here I am,*
a clearing.

~

Back to your nakedness and new love -
our eyes are melting,
our longing completed.

Feel
the compassion
rising from our chests,
the heat of our bodies
breathing *yes!*

Laughing *yes.*
Shouting *yes!*

So much through the night,
that a new universe bursts open,
and our baggage becomes light!

~

Now we return,
we come back.

To the reader,
and the *read*.

To the *words*,
and *what's being said.*

Back to games,
and mirrors.

Back to silent wanting and
hunger for everything else.

These days that go by, events unfolding
like a checkers match....

I know the garden I'm tending to.
So life reveals itself
in a lover's pocket watch....

Time to *get to it!*
Time to get so close that it hurts,
so close that it hurts so much that
it starts to feel good, so good that
you revive the self from slumber!

The loving begins!

We start now to rock,
we create a circle
and *breathe into a drum!*

We make love so passionately
that we become a song
that love put on!

~

At this point you're either
salivating or
dropping these words and meanings.

So if you're listening,
and if you're hungry,

put these words down anyway and
turn,
turn into yourself.

Pull,
like a warrior*!*

All the goodness and grace
that you could ever reach for
back into this world.

That way your lighter self may lie beside mine,
and we make love in that brightness,
in that depth of otherworldliness.

So a kiss
becomes a new sky,
a new friendship,

and the doorway
to a new
way

of being.

Essences

She -
The
essence
of understatement.

Me -
The
essence
of overstatement.

She moves silently,
peeling away the layers.

I thunder in loudly
and rip away your veils.

Magnetism with
hungry eyes?

Or a fashion show
and then goodbye?

I am a *yes*
or *no*.

Tomorrow will tell me
which one
is *so*.

So Reveals

What is art?
What is poetry?
What rides the rising wave?

I laughed and
in another poem
said sex -

to *climax*,
to build up an
infinite blazing energy in the body

and release it,
sing it back
into the universe!

Now that's all anyone ever cared about -
the *giving away*
and yet the *getting back!*

Of *surrendering*
the body
to another universe,

to another lover who
so reveals
the secret in you!

Love Wrestling

I am an invitation.
Again and again,
I invite.

No more obligations!
No more longing!

Only -
inciting the whole universe
into passion and lovemaking.

Stop caring
about the yes
or no!

Just ask!
Just make the *request to love!*

End every foolish game
that makes your loving so hard.

Loving is never hard,
yet longing is always hard
because of our wanting!

Loving comes from wanting.
Loving also comes from God.
But loving can come from wanting, which means -
You are *trying to get something with your love!*

What a weak force!
What a lie of a word!

Love, love, love,
I have heard it used before -

Like a knife,
like a net.

And even me,
my lover has been falling, falling.

With my lies I made her trip,
and with my hollow word
still claim to catch her?

What is the difference between love,
and everything less than it?

It's like seeing a beautiful woman for the first time -

Is it the beauty of her aliveness,
or her breasts,
that steers you here?

Can you justify
the way they sway
and her laughter

with loving her movement
and all beyond it?

I have seen everything lost
in the word love,
and yet still we are here,
growing, uncertain.

Uncertain
not only of where we come from,
who we are,
and what in the future will
make us happy....

My friends,
my lovers,
my enemies,

there is no such thing as time.

There is only
waking up
and falling asleep
continuously.

And how we move through space
we call time.

Really.

Dancing through space
or silence.

And the dancing
literally births
your experience.

So as your body spins,
its circuits and electrons
and brain and heart

swaying, breathing,

this is it,
we are *here* -

I whisper
"Give me your all,
or go back to sleep!"

How shall you undress?
How would you like to dance?

In my loving quiet
I am watching your moves,
so that we learn to become one,
the way we whirl.

We kindle each other's longing
and burn away the wanting.

Keep going, keep going,
until there's nothing left but

one consciousness
and
love wrestling!

All I Want

I want to *inspire her,*
that's all.

Like giving her a seed
and saying
plant it.

Plant it anywhere you want
and *it will grow.*

I go my way
and still love her.

Years go by,
the sun pulling us forward,

and I return to see her body
radiating the harvest -

love,
compassion,
sensuality.

She's breath-taking,
glowing,
channeling another world's eyes
down to this one.

And that,
dear friends,
is all I want.

The Whole World on Fire

She put up a wall.
I climbed over it.

It goes like this
forever -

Hearts build homes,

and even *they*
cover the
sky.

So *here I am* -

An effulgent stream
pouring into
the crevices
of your body-

I seep through your shields -
your pretenses.

Where the gap greets your essence,
I am standing there.

I am waiting
like a silent knowing.

And I am hungry, happily,
like a family breaking bread together
in the morning sun.

~

She comes to me apologizing,
saying words like
"falling apart" and "messy."

I respond,
the foundation
of my love-practice
is as follows:

To say the Name
and *remember*.

To *remember*

is to cast
your *self*
into God,

which is the state of
truth,
consciousness,
and bliss!
Sat-cit-ananda.

This bliss inside of you
burns away
your falling apart

just as the sun
lights the whole world
on fire!

Why We Keep Breathing

The current that flows
through you
in certain states

reveals something.

That's why I keep asking,
"have you tried this concoction before?"

- The one that makes you feel
a new sense of perception,
a new sense of being -
That's the one, that's the one I speak of.

How is it that
one minute we are looking at our world,
and another -

The world spins and breathes
in and out of us?

I look at the clouds and see
skeletons breathing,
living skeletons,
saying life breathes before you,
see the root, see the frame.

One minute I am breathing with this sky breath,
and another -
touch tastes like orgasm!

I am touching my skin,
I am stroking your hair
and longing to kiss my friends.

Let us *declare wildly*
null and void
the boundaries we left minutes ago

and stampede over them
in a love circus!

I have kissed many beautiful women this way.

But we weren't just kissing,
we were opening.

We said to each other,
you are so beautiful
in your *human being-ness,*
in your skin and eyes and tongue.

We gazed into each other's eyes
brimming with ecstasy,
heart drumming,
body breathing yes,

and kissed each other.
Sometimes passionately, sometimes delicately,
always joyfully, we giggled, we cast our eyes around the room
to discover the rest of our friends

swaying,
rolling on the waves
like us.

~

And then we wake up
to what scientists like to call
"ordinary consciousness."

Ha.

Now that the doorway has been opened,
now that a secret has been revealed...

Who is with me??

Who will wander back
to the other side?

It's not that I have the answers,
but that I am holding steadily
a blazing torch inside,

to light our way,
to light us lovers up,

and remind us all
why,

why we keep breathing!

Kissed by the Sun

One,
two,
three,

they fall
before
me.

Love does that,
love wipes you to your feet.

Our bodies pull,
our souls lull,
and our hearts
roar
into oblivion.

I am attacking your walls!
I am coming after you, finally!

I know that you have been waiting.

A sign,
a new sun,
and a question?

I am asking you
into me.

So the veils drop like clothes
and you listen closely
in our peaceful quiet.

I tell you,
love communicates
like water molecules.

So here I am,
bubbling up inside!

Aching to reveal
this radiating fountain of light
pouring from the center of my chest!

It springs forth
from this love connection -

This sacred bond
between us -

Between one human being,
and another answering:

I am here.
I am ready to love you.

So please
look into me,
sweet dear,

and come,
feed
from these ancient eyes!

Mirror of Fire

When we are alone,
sometimes
we feel our emptiness.

It greets us as a lonely desk,
a cold bed,
or an old memory
that still scars.

The meaninglessness of life haunts us before we sleep.
Yet again we rise and return
to the same isles, the same shallow voices and cracked paint.

Where is my benefactor and my brotherhood, we wonder?

Those with hollow faith sleep soundly
but wake and live in hate.
Those who ponder
know that life is married to suffering.

When we feel our emptiness, the heart can break,
but it can also mend.
To take on our suffering is to join hands with the world,
for every man weeps when he finds himself alone.
To join hands with the world is to embrace love over selfishness.
Only the selfish can know suffering.
To embrace love is to end war and begin healing the soul.

Our hearts are heavy with forgetfulness,
and these days which mix with grief and pain are full of sleep.
Still we move about, hoping to rise above what we do not
understand.

In another's eyes we find something beyond ourselves,
we see a mirror of fire.
And so we hatch a foolish plan to stop and catch a lover.
Yet the heat comes from within, and as we wait, this warmth we
dissipate.

We cannot run from the responsibilities of life,
but only transcend them by becoming stronger.
So then the fire grows and our fears burn away.

Finally,
when I am alone,
You pass by.

Your eyes ignite a flame that melts me from the inside.
Our hearts meet and for the first time I know peace.

The brotherhood is found.
The benefactor is alive and well.

The story ends as it begins -
a mystery rising from silence.

The sky stretches over us,
and the sun sets in majesty.

Book II
~
Love is a Stranger

ॐ

Silence

Silence
burns.

Silence
is a space
some come to readily,

while others through sacrifice
find themselves
alone.

I have nothing
to say to you.

I don't know why,
just that i'm
staring into silence.

I think,
I love you,
but what *is* this?

The only way
to draw the line
is to halt
the expression of love.

Now some may say here
that loving lives
beyond bodies,

and real world actions
are the essence.

But if you are waiting for an answer,
if you are looking for proof,
then be silent and stay that way,

because nothing I ever do or say
will open up your soul or mouth

except

my body
breathing love
into you.

A Book of Love

I want her body.
I want her body's longing,
her softness, her shape.

Yet she comes to me distantly,
wavering with
wary eyes.

I want to swallow whole
her fear and kiss away
her sadness.

All this wanting burns.
She knows the past,
I know the future.

This attempt at love -
Me breathing deeply in her presence,
her dancing closer, wondering
what's next....

~

I go away for many months.

Each day I
craft carefully
words for her nutrition.

Waiting for the day
to again feed her,

to again stoke a flame
that has flickered
in thoughtlessness -

Waiting to come to her,
waiting to come
with a book
bound by her moving me,

with a book of love
that can actually transform the world
and our turning inside of each other.

I want her love
to light up the world
like the sun!

We capture it,
soak it in,
until our bodies bronze
and moisten,

become pure, clay vessels
of love and strength
and freedom.

Intimacy is like a Secret

Intimacy
is like a secret.

If someone were to see,
if someone were to find out....

How shocking!
Such an uproar
would ensue!

How dare they do *that*,
with *them!*

The final frontier
is the soul squeezing
into the body.

So the most sacred
way to give yourself may be
to unveil the body's longing

in a twisting, wrestling,
moaning, sucking, kissing,
licking, touching
explosive act!

All in the name of love.

So that by the time you're through,
the other body is
ready for the secret-
ready to be whispered into.

Let's pretend we just made love
and we're at that moment:

Your heart beating,
your body smiling,
love oozing from every pore....

Silently I whisper,

"You are the universe. You are the seed.
See past your body! See past your self!
Remember the essence in every being,
and love unconditionally
until you reach remembrance."

~

You fall asleep,
then wake up
hours later,
dazed.

Can you bring that back?
Or shall you carelessly
again put on your clothes?

And forget the hidden meaning -
(which is why people get so angry)

*Nakedness
is truth.*

Love is sex.

Sex is a reminder
that God pushes past

into a space where sex
becomes the holy act of

creating and sustaining
a hundred million billion
universes!

Bow to the Moon

She opens

then
closes -

Asks
herself
away from me.

This space
steals away
so suddenly!

I am lightness,
then darkness.

A rising flame,
then smoke.

Her distance - I choke.
Her closeness - I awoke
for a moment.

For a moment
I moved into her

like a bee
does with a flower.

Her sweetness my nutrition,
yet too much becomes attrition.

I now know
when it's time to close.

Watch how
the sun burns
through the whole sky

then
bows out
to the moon.

Look around,
flowers grow everywhere.

They are opening and closing
every second
in the wind.

She is one of them,
swaying.

~

I come to you,
striding in from
the early morning fields
saying,

"Good news
my friends.

Wake up,
it's spring!"

The Equinox

What is love?
I am broken open,
I am a restless fever

as I watch my lover,
my old lover,
loving someone new.

What is love?
Does it demand
that all the veils be drawn?

Or is there a science
to the unveiling?

This is happening now,
this choice of
stepping into the fire,
or not.

Can I raise her up,
so that she invites me inside,
or is that not the final truth?

Is that a barrier
to loving
her loving of another?

I see the planets
spinning in her eyes,
I see her falling.

And I fall with her,
I fall into her again,
like it's the first time.

The jealous rage
of the past dissipates.

Here there is mostly
my sadness asking,

"Why aren't you living
the life you love,
so that she can be there with you,
loving your creation?"

This pouring out of light
and meeting so many
beautiful souls

is an ancient practice,
an ancient calling,
an ancient secret.

I love you,
I love this test,
I love this impossible feat
to which we must rise

with all the courage
and strength
and skill

that it will take
to heal a mad and hungry
world like this!

Swaying, Saying Thank You

Thank you.
I am saying thank you
at the beginning,
at the end,
thank you.

Pausing, thanking,
loving, thinking
thank you.

Look at me,
look at my mistakes.
Where does this madness
come from?

Why am I like an animal,
pacing, hunting
to kill something?

When really I am hunting
the hurt in my heart
that makes me feel

this.

I am sorry.
I am so sorry!
Thank you, thank you
for being you.

Thank you, Jackie, for your steady light,
I love you and hope this finds you all right.
Thank you for your wise compassion.

I am sorry for my lacking,
for my laziness,
for my willingness

to let it all go
for a state of being,
for escape of being.

Action.
I need action.
It's opening.
Up for me. Up for us
and the rest.

So *thank you.*
Thank you for remembering,
thank you for apologizing
for forgetting.

Sigh.

A weight
in my chest.

The first sign
that this bursting
is not pure light.

~

I ask the universe -
now, in this moment,

can I see my mistakes
and become free from them?

Please take away my lust,
please higher Self.

Take away my empty hunger
but leave me with the burning
that will purify my longing.

No more vain self,
let's let the love of God in.

Forget the sex,
see the sexiness.
See past the body.

See the soul swaying sweetly and smile,
smile, say thank you,
and feel alive.

Love is a Stranger

Such sadness
wrapped in such glory,

stainless, infinite Spirit
resigned to these pitiful situations,

in some ways
crushed by the weight
of earth's reflections.

I have seen in dreams
the world full of love and light.
I have seen the way
we smile and get on.

Yet I wake up to this violence,
this separation -
love and *war*.

Love knows no violence,
so how does it conquer?

Violence derives from vacuousness,
where love has not yet bloomed.

So all love has to do
is spread its seed -
plant itself in the hungry fields
and grow.

That's where you and I come in,
we bridges of
body-spirit.

We must be planting fervently,
endlessly, steadily,
on a mission to
incite the world to love.

Who has done this?
The great beings
of the world.

You think of Jesus and Muhammad,
I name Buddha and Lao Tzu.
There are too many to count.

They cry out to us,
they remind us -
this is not the life!

The life is love,
an endless lesson!

Bow down to it!
Bow down to what you love!

But each day I wake up
with a task list,
a do-this to become-that.

This is the way we live,
bartering our goals and strategies
like wares in the market.

Yet to wake up and
bow like the trees....
This is the only way!

How does one
let loose
the spirit that resides
inside these
clay shells?

Gratitude.

Which means mouthfuls of
please, or
thank you, or
listening, or
being sorry.

~

As I see the stars
spin in your eyes

and wonder
about my origin,
the root of this
body-spirit,

I know that
love
is a stranger.

I keep praying
that one day
love will knock on my door
and take me home.

This Love Planet

"All of your sorrow exists for one reason - that you may end sorrow
forever." - Rumi

~

These nights I sit alone,
waiting,
listening,
suspicious of the universe,
God is moving
through me.

All along I'm angry,
or sad,
or tired,
because my love
veils itself.

When will I learn
that my burning is yearning
for something else,
something deeper?

It is time to shed our layers.
It is time to let go of our grief,
unless it is for God.

Grief for God, forget the rest.
Everything else is childish.

Grief that I am stuck here
breathing heavily,
seemingly pulled down
by the world.

Purify yourself!
Feel the blood rushing through your veins!
Build your muscles stronger!
Breathe deeply
and find your rhythm.

Eat like
you love light.
Stop following strange diets.

Stop setting yourself up
to trip, to fall,
to plan in the distance.

Do it now!

Get down on your knees,
bow your head low,
and pray to God!

Pray to this infinite universe!
Give up knowing and being
anything other than
light pouring in and out
of your spirit!

Let us ready ourselves,
let us gather round the sacred spaces.

Let us breath God,
let us chant God,
let our voice become
God speaking.

La ilaha ilallah!
La ilaha ilallah!

There is no reality but God!
There is no-*thing*. There is only God!

Every time you imagine something violent,
repent.
Let God wash over you.

Every time you feel full of joy and gratitude,
give thanks!
Let God wash over you.

Every time you succeed,
praise God!

Every time you fail,
praise God!

Let us keep remembering
that we are here, in a world
of sleeping sadness,

but we come from
the *planet of love*.

I am readying myself,
rotating my spirit around
this *love-planet*.

Moving closer,
moving closer,
to *pure spirit!*

Book III

~

The World of Love

ॐ

We Can go so Far

So much gathering can be done
by reaching out,
out to your neighbors.

And so much gathering can be done
by reaching out,
reaching with your heart.

I sit alone
for many months
and some scratch their heads at me,
not knowing the gift of
silence and separation.

The holy words begin
reminding us of our separation,
this division between
body and *spirit.*

We can go
so far
when we turn off the senses.

So far
that we stumble upon the heart,
which veils the soul,
which veils pure spirit.

I move through You
to discover hidden worlds.

You -
The invisible,
silent,
all-pervading.

You -
the flavor of life itself,
love's passion
wrapped in ecstasy.

How I long for you!

How I long for the highest truth,
the highest mastery,
the highest realization!

Remembering this taste
means making love
to infinity!

Otherwise
I am out in the world
grasping on to beautiful objects -
desiring them, hunting them,
gathering.

Look what I've found!
We've shouted a million times.
We're still looking, still hungry.

Watch as these words
wash over
in waves,

they move perspectives
like writing on the wall.

Let's start a new story.

When everything outside is falling down,
when the whole world begins to rise in flames,

we cultivate the essence of a true human being -

Love
at any cost.

~

When Hallaj shouted,
"I am the Truth!"
they beheaded him
for heresy.

Gods are crossing the doorsill
every second
getting slaughtered.

They will never stop,
they will never stop
coming into us.

Friends,
our human history sees us
shedding many skins,
many layers of forgetfulness.

We are now ready
for another peel,
another collective tearing away
of the veil.

Reach out with your heart
and discover the center,

discover the eternal life
that blooms when
living in love.

No more doors,
no more crossing over,
no more separation.

Only freedom.
Only bliss.

Only the universe
sparkling in your eyes.

Only blank pages
that blink with words.

Words
that can heal
the world.

The World of Love

Why have we cultivated
our currency in coins? When
we are living for *love!*

It's forged at a higher temperature.

The choice now is
love or gold.

No exceptions.

The world we want
comes from love,

the hell we've inherited -
built on empty coins.

No longer, my friend.

The world is on fire
and the flames
will melt everything away but
You.

The *love* in you -
The *personification* of love.
The experience, the act,
the *moving through.*

They will melt away your fears and
forgetfulness and treasons,
your sorrows and empty reasons...

Love or gold?

It's so easy to decide
once you've burned away
the veils.

After they threw me in the pot,
I rose to a higher existence.

This is a bridge,
this love-connection.

One by one
we will love everyone.
One by one
love will lure you across.

Show me a man
who would choose money over love,
and I will fight him to the death
and win.

That is love-conversion.
(The death isn't really real.)

Me telling you how happy I am to see you,
me holding your hands and
gazing into your eyes...
this is love-connection.

You remembering joy
with your body and breath and
whole emotion-
love conversations...

About who made the sky
and who painted colors
onto these beach-bronzed eyes
that echo the sound of waves
in your heart,

expanding
and fading,
and running onto the shore
like a slow waking up,

a waking up and into
the world
of love.

I am like a Flame

Meditate
every day.

About an hour each
should do.

Seriously.

You'll start to feel a shiver
that moves like a lightning bolt
where the whole sky is brooding
and pours itself onto your floor!

Listen,
can listening ever get you back to
why you hear?

Feel me,
can this touch
ever bring you back
to the source?

Watch me move,
can my iridescence cause you
to spark too?

I am like a flame
that flickers longingly

to light the whole world
on fire!

And you are dry wood,
we are kindling,
gathered here.

So *burn, baby, burn!*

Let's let the world
live the way
we love to!

In this ever-expanding experience
of peace, love, joy, and the
sexiest intelligence
anyone ever spoke of.

So meditate,
my dear,
and *breathe.*

Breathe until
you *become*
this fire
with me!

The Only Conspiracy I Believe In

The only conspiracy
I believe in
is *love*.

Love plotting
day and night

to overturn every single table
that you set through life

that was fancied out of
anything less
than love.

Are we still talking about
a conspiracy?

Opening into Love

The senses reflect
what they receive.

So love keeps smattering itself
against your windshield,
waiting for you to take notice.

Like the sun,
love waits and warms you
whether or not you have learned
to feel the heat.

Life gifts itself to us
every moment,

and our senses struggle
to soak this in -

Scrambling to recreate
the glory that is

opening into love.

The Color of your Soul

No more bold statements,
no more fancy claims,
only circling.

Can you feel me
being picked up by the wind
and carried?

Carried here,
to you, like this,
in our time of need?

What do you really want in life?

Give me your hunger or your death.
They are really the same and either will do.
One leads to becoming, the other to letting go.

If you find yourself blank, empty of life's passions,
I will kiss your eyes and watch you fall back asleep.

If you find yourself suffering, churning with emotion,
brimming with something, even if it isn't joy,

come to me.
I will open your windows.

First though I will humbly
knock on your doors.

That's what's happening here - this preparation.
Every angle must be approached, every way weighted.

Self-mastery enlivens every aspect of human experience,
so I can discover my way into the color of your soul.

In other words,
you hear me knocking.

*All you want
is to love and be loved.*

The rest is broken language.

As I start to speak in our ancient tongue,
we will, like lovers,
rediscover infinity
in our own home.

Aching for Perfection

Every part of you
is *aching*
for perfection.

Aching
to *return* to perfection,
to *embody* it.

Every crevice of yours
is waiting,
hungry for light.

The torchbearers are coming.

Soon the whole sky
will light up,

and we will
become one

and

*merge with
the sun!*

We are the Architects of a New World

I have no type,
we have no home.

We live in the building bridges
between our destiny and
this current state.

One of them is a curtain,
the other a blazing glory.

~

We are the architects
of a new world,

where love leaps
into real space!

I am a miracle,
we are, this birth.

Come with me and dance
like you are on fire,
like you have something to say!

- Born again
every moment of being

and can't help but inspire us all
to fall in love with you!

To Be a Lover

You don't have to be smart
to be a lover,

you just have to
love.

Inducing Ecstasy

I am inducing
ecstasy
in my veins.

I am rising
my spirit

like a making love
to existence.

~

This study I am
embarking on

is the study of
the funnel of light.

There is a ladder.
This way has already been
emblazoned.

~

Come with me
and rediscover

the meaning
and secret
of being
alive!

All I Talk About

All I talk about
is love.

I recently discovered
that there's nothing else.

Science and other words
wander paradoxes.

Love cuts through,
slices straight into the source.

Tell me everything you love,
and I will gather your telling.

Tell me what you fear, your anger,
I will gather all of that too.

The first basket
is for burning.

Your love becomes incense,
a prayer, raised into the sky.

The second basket also burns.

This suffering becomes a cleansing,
a letting go of the past.

Here's what I've gathered:

First,
please drop every negative thought
that's ever been.

Second,
please never pick back up
any of them *ever again.*

You're built for
so much more.

Last,
with each and every breath,

give your love
to the world.

The Way your Body Moves

No machine is as delicate
as the human spirit,

the human hand that pens
the words *"I love you."*

No fineness of detail
ever legitimizes automating value.

Values live between breaths,
not in the hum of dumb matter.

See that meaninglessness,
and see your longing for love
and living fully.

Embrace that longing
so that you pay more attention
to the way your body moves,

and the way the universe
mirrors
to greet you!

When You Start Loving Everyone

There *is* a hierarchy of love.

We have to keep climbing,
even though it hurts.

When you learn
to let go of your identity,
you discover that
there is no separation.

This conversation, that river,
you and me,

us staring at each other
in all these different ways,

peering into new worlds
that we can't even see...

You are the *lover* and the *loved*.
You are beyond being both.
You are *one.*

You are the essence!

Which means that you are becoming God
and that you are God -

all the while trapped
in your *mind's body,*

instead of participating wholly
in this world's rising!

So when you start to love me,
drop the veils
and *see the becoming!*

Your longing
turns to loving,

because
you *are what you love.*

When you start loving everyone,
the world gets
so much bigger!

Watch the universe expand
inside of you

and rise to the top
of the tallest mountain.

What a view!

We are silenced.

Go there.
Come here.
Now.

Shouting Land!

There's so much
that I haven't told you,
so much that I've forgotten
to do or say.

Like,
I love you.

I love you in whatever way
that you want to be loved.

It doesn't have to be serious,
or intimate, or near.
Love finds its course.

What I am saying is -
Whatever you are lacking in life,

a bridge is being built inside me
to take you past your lacking,

to *carry you*
from this earthly danger
to the heavenly shore.

I have not arrived yet either,
but I can see the shore

and am shouting like Columbus
to every lover in the world,
"Land! Land! Land!"

Loving Reminders

Her beauty will not disappear.

The thing about life is that
we are given this gift,
this *present*,
that we don't understand.

When I see her,
I know that her beauty still lives,
still gives, even to the air,

and I bow down. Here, now,
I am bowing down.

Thank you for loving me then.
I didn't need it then, I don't need it now,
but you *reminded me.*

That's what the world needs -
loving reminders.

~

A beautiful day with friends,
a night of loving,
your happiest memories...

Let's *remember*
to love.

I Want the Whole Thing!

I don't want part of the truth, we say.

I want the whole thing!

When you are born into laughing
at all of your mistakes
such that you correct them,
the sun comes up differently.

No more parts, only wholes.
The clouds dance with you,
bowing in the sky.

You are more than you think you are,
and now I can prove it.

I am blessed with these blessings
that I bring to you.

Let me show you how to stretch,
how to bow,
how to breathe!

I can show you how to move.
What else are you looking for?

Stop looking for things
and find them!

It's like you keep knocking on my door
when I've already shouted
"Come in!"

So *come in*
to this house of loving,
and let us *live in love.*

Silence,
then laughter,
then a new kind of speaking.

The Final State

We are moving
toward something.

We are gathering round
a source,

gathering round
some force
like magnets.

I am here to remind you
why

and maybe even
what
this *is*.

~

We are crafting words
like escape rafts,
sailing into our dreams.

I see your hunger,
I see your longing,

and I am here with you,
hunting for survival.

Survival of the self,
survival of these impossible ideas
that we love to sleep with.

Like,
I want it to be this way always.
I want her to bend like this,
me live like that,
as in a picture.

Friends,
we are moving much faster
than the speed of light!

Please stop slowing down
to capture the beauty
you endlessly fall into.

Just keep falling.

There is an end-point,
this is a well,
we are getting closer.

~

Night comes,
and we throw off our robes
in celebration.

But what are we celebrating?
Do we forget the reasons why we live,
and join the wild animals
in a free for all?

Or are we *remembering*,
and therefore casting off our chains?

Living our lives
like blacksmiths -
Hammering away,

striking fearlessly a new way
free from shackles!

These nights you sit in the shop,
keep practicing,
keep practicing,
we are getting closer.

~

The *why* is this:
Imagine if everything you loved
loves you back!

This is the final truth.

The *what* is this:
Your body is a vessel,
but you are the current.
You are the entire universe!

And you would get this,
and you would *live* this,
if you could speed up and slow down
at the same time.

But since time is short,
and I am almost through,
the last words spill onto the pages
like this:

97

We are moving towards
a final state.

Love is the ship,
actions are the oars,
and I am your captain,
calling to you,

"Keep breathing!
Keep pushing your self to expand!"

So that we reach the shore together,
we sail straight into heaven,

like lovers
holding hands
on a full moon.

At peace, at rest,
and yet
making love endlessly
like radiant,
blooming stars!

Epilogue

ॐ

I Hope To Meet You Soon

Whomever the universe
brings to me,
I greet them.

All I have are
two open hands
and a basket.

The hands receive
while the basket gives.

Who is filling up my basket,
you ask?
I don't know!

Who do *you*
say it is?

Lo, I call it *God!*
I call it *Love!*

I call it these words
that wrap around your waist
and whisper longingly,
"love me!"

Love me
any way you want,
as long as you love me.

This community creates continuously
a beautiful circle

of people moving,
people living,

people loving
past their oldness.

Love on,
fellow traveler.

Know that I hope
to meet you soon!

Thank you for reading this book!

~

Thank you Isabelle Crow for editing this book and recreating these poems afresh with me!

Thank you Brenda Clark and Katya Walter for editing this book and sharing your wisdom with me.

Thank you for inspiring these poems:
Mom, Dad, Jackie Sy, Kelsey Crow, Isabelle Crow, Valentina, Paulina...Blessings to you all.

Thank you beautiful poets of the world!
Chief inspirations being Rumi, Hafiz, Mary Oliver, Billy Collins...

~

Please let me know how you feel:
rumisroses@gmail.com

Love!
Peter